LEAP OVER A WALL
STUDY GUIDE

LEAP OVER A WALL
STUDY GUIDE

EARTHY SPIRITUALITY FOR EVERYDAY CHRISTIANS

EUGENE H. PETERSON

NAVPRESS

Discipleship Inside Out™

NavPress is the publishing ministry of The Navigators, an international Christian organization and leader in personal spiritual development. NavPress is committed to helping people grow spiritually and enjoy lives of meaning and hope through personal and group resources that are biblically rooted, culturally relevant, and highly practical.

For a free catalog go to www.NavPress.com
or call 1.800.366.7788 in the United States or 1.800.839.4769 in Canada.

ISBN-13: 978-1-61747-159-9

Cover illustrations by Shutterstock

Study guide by Neil Wilson

Some of the anecdotal illustrations in this book are true to life and are included with the permission of the persons involved. All other illustrations are composites of real situations, and any resemblance to people living or dead is coincidental.

Unless otherwise identified, all Scripture quotations in this publication are taken from the *THE MESSAGE* (MSG). Copyright © 1993, 1994, 1995, 1996, 2000, 2001, 2002. Used by permission of NavPress Publishing Group. Other versions used include: The Holy Bible, English Standard Version (ESV), copyright © 2001 by Crossway Bibles, a division of Good News Publishers. Used by permission. All rights reserved; the *Holy Bible, New International Version®* (NIV®), Copyright © 1973, 1978, 1984 by International Bible Society, used by permission of Zondervan, all rights reserved; and the *Revised Standard Version Bible* (RSV), copyright 1946, 1952, 1971, by the Division of Christian Education of the National Council of the Churches of Christ in the USA, used by permission, all rights reserved.

Printed in the United States of America

1 2 3 4 5 6 7 8 / 16 15 14 13 12 11

CONTENTS

WELCOME

If you want to get to know someone, one effective approach is to spend time with those around that person. The impression one person leaves on others often gives us a clearer picture of him than we may perceive on our own. Think about that the next time you list names under "references" on a job description.

Leap Over a Wall allows us to get to know David, son of Jesse of Bethlehem, who became king of Israel, by looking at the people and events that influenced him the most. These were also people whose lives were radically altered because of David.

The phrase that serves as the title of this book was expressed by David in Psalm 18 as a way of describing the effect of God's presence in his life:

> *For it is you who light my lamp;*
> > *the LORD my God lightens my darkness.*
> *For by you I can run against a troop,*
> > *and by my God I can leap over a wall.*
> *This God—his way is perfect;*
> > *the word of the LORD proves true;*
> > *he is a shield for all those who take refuge in him.*
> (Psalm 18:28-30, ESV, emphasis added)

As we visit with the crowd of witnesses from David's life, we will learn that David meant every phrase of this personal confession. Notice that while David credited God for allowing several things he could do (run against a troop; leap over a wall), he also listed many more things

God did for him that he couldn't do for himself (light his lamp, lighten his darkness, provide a perfect way and a true word, and shield him). David knew that even leaping over a building in a single bound didn't in any way diminish his need for God's daily presence in his life.

As for us, we will need God's help to leap over those walls that stand between us and David's life. Tall structures of spiritualization and perfectionism have created a Bible person with whom we could never share anything in common. Those walls have been erected over the centuries and we are not likely to make much progress in tearing them down. We might as well count on God to help us leap over them. This study comes with a prayer that it will lift your life and be used by God's Spirit to do all for you that God was willing to do for David.

HOW TO USE THIS REFLECTIVE STUDY GUIDE

First, read each chapter of *Leap Over a Wall* before you undertake the corresponding study of the chapter. As Eugene Peterson explains in the first chapter, let the David story sink a little deeper into your life before you start looking at that particular episode from that story in more detail.

Second, note the structure of the chapter-lessons. After reminding you to read the chapter, the reflection tools will follow this outline:

- Read—A Scripture and a book chapter to experience
- Theme Word—The recurring idea from David's story
- Key Passages—Related passages for further study
- David's Story—Quotes from *Leap Over a Wall* and questions to explore particular events, moments, and places in the David story
- Larger Story—Quotes from *Leap Over a Wall* and questions to explore the wider and longer implications of the lessons from David's story
- Your Story—Quotes from *Leap Over a Wall* and questions designed to help you integrate the discoveries from David's story into your own story
- For Prayerful Reflection—Suggestions for a time to listen and respond to God speaking into your story

Third, interact with others about what you are discovering. Tell them the story of the David you're getting to know. Identify some of the characters in your life that have positive and negative roles similar to ones played by the people who influenced David.

Fourth and most important, give yourself to the same God who inhabited David's life. Let God saturate your story with his presence. And remember that the deepest lesson David learned was that the God who inhabited his life welcomed him to take refuge in him. The inhabiting went both ways. As David put it in Psalm 18:30, "This God . . . is a shield for all those who take refuge in him" (ESV).

STORIES

David and Jesus

READ

1 Samuel 16–1 Kings 2
Chapter 1, pages 1–11

THEME WORD: STORY

Though separated in time by almost a thousand years, the connections between David and Jesus were close in many ways. In human terms, Jesus was a son of David. The gospel of Matthew begins by establishing that lineage connection between the founder of the dynasty and the fulfillment of God's promise to that dynasty. The reign of Jesus ensures there will always be a king on the throne of David.

Eugene Peterson begins David's story with his own story. In particular, he explains his fascination with story, a gift spoken into his life by his mother. He points to her lively storytelling style as the source of his vivid recollections.

KEY PASSAGES

Oh yes, you shaped me first inside, then out;
you formed me in my mother's womb.
I thank you, High God—you're breathtaking!
Body and soul, I am marvelously made!

I worship in adoration—what a creation!
You know me inside and out,
  you know every bone in my body;
You know exactly how I was made, bit by bit,
  how I was sculpted from nothing into something.
Like an open book, you watched me grow from conception to birth;
  all the stages of my life were spread out before you,
The days of my life all prepared
  before I'd even lived one day. (Psalm 139:13-16)

The Word was first,
  the Word present to God,
  God present to the Word.
The Word was God,
  in readiness for God from day one. . . .
The Word became flesh and blood,
  and moved into the neighborhood.
We saw the glory with our own eyes,
  the one-of-a-kind glory,
  like Father, like Son,
Generous inside and out,
  true from start to finish. (John 1:1-2,14)

1 Samuel 16–1 Kings 2
Psalm 8; 23; 139

DAVID'S STORY

1. Note below the first five facts about David of Israel that come to
your mind from past exposure to his story.

“ Story is the primary way in which the revelation of God is given to us. . . . From beginning to end, our Scriptures are primarily written in the form of story. . . . And the Holy Spirit weaves all this storytelling into the vast and holy literary architecture that reveals God to us as Father, Son, and Holy Spirit in the way that he chooses to make himself known. Story. To get this revelation right, we enter story ” (page 3).

2. It has been said that the Bible is not so much history as his-story. How have you experienced the power of story in your inter-action with the Scriptures?

3. At this point, what is your understanding of the connections between King David of Israel and Jesus of Nazareth?

4. Who taught you that connection, and how did they do it?

“ The David story is the most extensively narrated single story in this large story. We know more about David than any other person in Holy Scripture ” (page 3).

5. In relation to the other people in the Bible, how much do you know about David?

6. What would be one personal question that you would like answered as you explore the David story in this book?

LARGER STORY

" Story is the primary way in which the revelation of God is given to us " (page 3).

7. How does Peterson explain and expand what he means by this statement?

8. What difference does it make if we look at the Bible as story?

" Life isn't an accumulation of abstractions such as love and truth, sin and salvation, atonement and holiness; life is the realization of details that all connect organically, personally, specifically: names and finger-prints, street numbers and local weather, lamb for supper and a flat tire in the rain. God reveals himself to us not in a metaphysical formu-lation or a cosmic fireworks display but in the kind of stories that we use to tell our children who they are and how to grow up as human beings, tell our friends who we are and what it's like to be human " (page 3).

9. What is your favorite children's story? What does it teach about being human?

10. Why is it important not to try to reduce life to abstractions, but to see it and experience it as a dynamic flow?

YOUR STORY

" We can't get away from God; he's there whether we like it or not, whether we know it or not. We can refuse to participate in God; we can act as if God weren't our designer, provider, and covenant pres-ence. But when we refuse, we're less; our essential humanity is less. Our lives are diminished and impoverished " (page 6).

11. How would you describe the current state of your awareness of God in and around your life? In what way does that presence make you "more"?

12. What does Peterson say to you about the role the David story can play in alerting us to "God-dimensional humanity" (page 6)? How does this intrigue you?

" A surprising thing about the readers of this [Jesus] story is that, by and large, through the Christian centuries, we've had a harder time taking seriously the human elements of the story than the divine. It's been easier to believe that Jesus was God than that Jesus was human **"** (page 7).

13. How does this tension affect you? Does Jesus inhabit your life as Man, God, or the unique God-Man who refuses to be separated? And what difference does it make to you?

14. As you begin this study, the discipline of reading the corresponding Bible passages as well as the chapter from *Leap Over a Wall* will significantly impact the benefits you will receive from spending time in the David story. And it may well cause you to

think of the Jesus story in ways you haven't thought before. What is one personal expectation you have for this study?

FOR PRAYERFUL REFLECTION

These reflection moments may be life-changing for you. Set aside enough time when you do the lesson to consider these opportunities on your own as well as with the group you may be meeting with. This is the time to deliberately invite God to add what you have just studied to the ingredients he is using to shape your life. Take a moment to ask him to give you a fresh heart and fresh eyes to see David in his story, and then see your own story with new eyes.

NAMES

David and Samuel

READ

1 Samuel 16:1-13
Chapter 2, pages 13–24

THEME WORD: NAMES

How can there be stories without names? Names help us keep the characters sorted out; Bible names often become linked with character. Before we meet David in the Bible, we meet Samuel. Like many biblical names, the "el" at the end points to God—a shortened, careful form of one of God's names, *elohim*. Samuel means "heard of God," a name his mother Hannah chose to celebrate that his birth was an answer to prayer. Samuel plays a unique role for God in David's life.

1. What is the story behind your name?

KEY PASSAGES

As it is, your kingly rule is already falling to pieces. GOD is out looking for your replacement right now. This time he'll do the choosing. When

*he finds him, he'll appoint him leader of his people. And all because you
didn't keep your appointment with GOD!* (1 Samuel 13:14)

Exodus 19:6
1 Samuel 16:1-13

DAVID'S STORY

2. What was Samuel's state of mind as he started out to identify
and anoint God's choice for a replacement for King Saul?
(See 1 Samuel 16:1-5.)

3. Why was there a certain amount of danger in Samuel's assign-
ment, and how was that danger minimized? (See 1 Samuel 16:1-5.)

" As it turns out, and as the whole world now knows, there was another
son, David. But he enters the story unnamed, dismissively referred to
by his father as 'the baby brother'—in Hebrew, *haqqaton*, the youngest, in effect saying: 'Well, there's the baby brother, but he's out tend-
ing the sheep' (1 Sam. 16:11 [RSV]). If you're the youngest of seven
brothers, you're probably never going to be thought of as other than
the kid brother. *Haqqaton* carries undertones of insignificance, of not
counting for very much—certainly not a prime candidate for presti-
gious work. The family runt " (page 16).

4. First Samuel 16:10 tells us seven sons were available for presen-
tation, not busy doing other things. David had to be summoned.

What might this tell you about his acceptance of his role in the family?

5. Peterson points out that in the larger scheme of things, "it's unlikely that anyone in Bethlehem that day 'saw' the anointing" (page 17). If this event came off as publicly insignificant, then what does the account tell us was the purpose of Samuel's visit? (See 1 Samuel 16:13.)

❝ In this narration of the selection and anointing of David, his personal name is withheld until the very end (v. 13), giving it a special place of prominence. . . .

David's name, not his role or position, is the final word in this initial story of his life ❞ (page 24).

6. Why is David's name important? What is the significance of names and their value? (See page 24.)

LARGER STORY

❝ It's highly significant and not sufficiently remarked that this David story, the story that provides more plot and detail, more characters and landscape than any other in Scripture to show us how to live entirely before and in response to God, features an ordinary person ❞ (page 17).

7. What specifics does Peterson point out that indicate David and his family might have been an entirely unexpected choice to supply royal material, and eventually the promised Savior? (See also Micah 5:2.)

8. Why was God's choice in this crucial historic moment "highly significant"?

66 David's life is the premier biblical instance of what's sometimes called 'the priesthood of all believers.' David's ancestors, freshly rescued from a doomed life in Egypt, heard the constituting sentence: 'You shall be to me a kingdom of priests' (Exod. 19:6 [RSV]). When that sentence struck their ears, they could only have reacted with a kind of uncomprehending astonishment 99 (page 19).

9. How does Peterson define the word *priest*? (See pages 20–21.)

10. In this sense, who can be priests?

11. The unlikely event of someone like David being tapped to be a king and also have a role as priest sets the stage for Peterson to write: "In the community of faith this 'bilevelism' is unacceptable. Biblically, there's unremitting war against it" (page 19). What "bilevelism" is he referring to, and why is it unacceptable?

YOUR STORY

" Throughout my childhood, in my mother's telling of the story, I became David. I was always David. I'm *still* David. It's the intent and skill of this scriptural storyteller to turn everyone who reads or hears the story into realizing something essentially Davidic about him- or herself: 'In my insignificant, sheep-keeping obscurity, I am chosen' " (page 17).

12. From what you know of David's story, how does this connection or identification ring true for you?

13. Considering the emphasis in this chapter on the potential priestly role of God's people, who would you say are the primary people in your life with whom God has called you to have a priestly role?

14. Who have been some of the Chet Ellingsons in your life? In what lives have you played that role?

❝ And I keep noticing the significance and spiritual force that these stories—these *lives!*—acquire when set in the context of the David story, a story that plunges us into the ordinary and saturates us in the everydayness in which the Holy Spirit is writing the story of *my, your, salvation* ❞ (page 23).

15. Based on this chapter, what would you say is the most significant thing about you?

FOR PRAYERFUL REFLECTION

Be quiet before God for a while and consider what it means that he knows your name, he knows you. Settle into the distinct possibility that he has a purpose for your life. You may never see that whole purpose this side of eternity. But while you wait for more understanding of God's purposes, focus on being grateful to God for working in and through your life.

WORK

David and Saul

READ

1 Samuel 16:14-23

Chapter 3, pages 25–34

THEME WORD: WORK

Work: Is it a curse or a calling? Do kings actually work? Do we work to live, or live to work—or maybe both? Because work and worship ultimately have something to do with God, how do we approach each of them? Outside the chores he did for his family, David's first job was for King Saul. That formal relationship provided the framework for the turbulent dealings between them. They both had work to do. Their story is a case study in work as a more or less effective expression of worship.

KEY PASSAGES

David came to Saul and stood before him. Saul liked him immediately and made him his right-hand man.

Saul sent word back to Jesse: "Thank you. David will stay here. He's just the one I was looking for. I'm very impressed by him."

After that, whenever the bad depression from God tormented Saul, David got out his harp and played. That would calm Saul down, and he would feel better as the moodiness lifted. (1 Samuel 16:21-23)

Genesis 1:1–2:4; 3:16-19
1 Samuel 10:27; 11:7; 13:13; 15:19; 16:14-23
Psalm 8:5-6
Luke 4:18

DAVID'S STORY

1. The encounter between Saul and David happens shortly after Samuel anoints the young shepherd boy. What condition in Saul's life brought the two together? (See 1 Samuel 16:14-23.)

2. What do we learn about David in this series of events, and what was the original tone of his relationship with Saul? (See 1 Samuel 16:14-23.)

" Somewhere along the line Saul's God-anointed work ceased to be an expression of God's sovereignty and became Saul's responsibility for sovereignty. The prevailing political model of kingship obliterated the prophetic model. The telling detail is that worship and work became two different things, one at the service of the other. The worship was undertaken so that the work would prosper. The consequence was fatal. (The reverse arrangement, work undertaken so that worship will prosper, is equally fatal.) **"** (page 27).

3. What was Saul's God-anointed work?

4. What does Peterson mean by "worship was undertaken so that the work would prosper"?

5. Why was Saul rejected by God? (See 1 Samuel 15:10.)

" Saul has made a mess of things. A royal mess. He had been given a job to do and had ruined it. David is now assigned to do well what Saul had done badly.

David was anointed by Samuel to be king, but he wasn't recognized as a king for another twenty years or so. . . .

His first job as a king was serving a bad king. . . . For David, serving was in itself ruling. The servant was simultaneously king. David in Saul's court was a king serving a king. Jesus, whom we worship as King, spent most of his life at the work of carpentry " (pages 32–33).

6. If serving under Saul was not an apprenticeship for David, what was it? (See page 31.)

7. From what you know of David's life, how did he serve Saul?

LARGER STORY

" God is first presented to us in our Scriptures as a worker, a maker. In the beginning, God went to work. . . . In the second creation story, man and woman are placed in the garden as workers, employed at tasks assigned by their maker (Gen. 2). Work is the primary context for our spirituality. . . .

Work is our Spirit-anointed participation in God's work **"** (page 27).

8. If work was the original context of the human relationship with God, and that didn't change with the fall of humanity into sin, then what did change about work as a result of the Fall? (See Genesis 3:16-19.)

9. On page 28, how does Peterson expand and apply the idea of anointment to work?

" What we're after is a seamless world of work and worship, worship and work. Only God is sovereign. Our work is derivative from God the worker **"** (page 27).

10. Why should we be aiming for an intertwined understanding of work and worship?

11. What happens when one of these eclipses the other?

" I want to use the word *kingwork* to represent all true work. I'm using this word in order to call attention to the essential dignity of work as such, to emphasize that our work is of a kind with God's work. All real work, genuine work, is subsumed under kingwork " (page 31).

12. What kinds of work wouldn't fit under the term *kingwork*? Why?

13. Peterson comes back to this idea of dignity when he says, "Dignity is inherent in work. Royalty is inherent in work. A major and essential task of the Christian is to recover work as vocation—as holy work. Every Christian takes holy orders" (page 32). Why do you think this is such a foreign concept among Christians?

YOUR STORY

14. What was your first real work experience? What taught you the meaning of work and how does your current attitude/ experience with work match what Peterson is describing?

15. How would you describe the worship aspect of your current work situation?

66 I've always counted myself fortunate in being brought up in an environment in which work and worship were virtually indistinguishable. Work and worship were aspects of one world. The world of work was a holy place for me 99 (page 28).

16. How do you relate to Peterson's description of the overlap and connections between work and worship in his father's butcher shop? (See pages 29–30.)

17. Later, Peterson says that as a pastor, "I found myself dealing with men and women who didn't know how to act in the place of worship" (page 30). How do you relate to his description of the problem and the solution he suggests?

66 Work can reveal something essential about us—express our values, articulate our morals, act out our convictions of what it means to be a human being, created in the image of God. Conversely, work can conceal our real identity; it can be used as a front to advertise something that we want people to see in us or believe about us but that in fact we've never bothered to become within ourselves 99 (page 33).

18. Which of these effects of work apply to your life? Why does Peterson point out that they are both often present?

19. What do you think would be at least one way that you could develop deeper integrity in the overlap between work and worship in your life?

FOR PRAYERFUL REFLECTION

Ask God to show you how you could worship while you work, and still work. Ask for an awareness of his presence and a growing sense that the command to pray without ceasing really does make sense, even at work.

IMAGINATION

David and Goliath

READ
1 Samuel 17
Chapter 4, pages 35–45

THEME WORD: IMAGINATION
Stories jump-start imagination, and a good story expands, deepens, and sharpens imagination. Resisting imagination's role makes us dull—dull company, even for ourselves. Imagination is a place in us where God expands our vistas in every direction, unless we are deliberate in locking him out.

1. Describe how David and Goliath look in your mental Photoshopped view.

KEY PASSAGES

"Because you're not yet taking God seriously," said Jesus. "The simple truth is that if you had a mere kernel of faith, a poppy seed, say, you

would tell this mountain, 'Move!' and it would move. There is nothing you wouldn't be able to tackle." (Matthew 17:20)

1 Samuel 17

DAVID'S STORY

2. What are Goliath and David busy doing in the hours before their encounter in the Valley of Elah?

3. In what way was each of these men prepared for this meeting? (See 1 Samuel 17:33-34.)

4. What moment in this episode from David's life is most vivid in your imagination? Why do you think that's the case?

❝My attention is caught and held by this wonderful but improbable scene: David on his knees at the brook; David kneeling and selecting five smooth stones, feeling each one, testing it for balance and size; David out in the middle of the Valley of Elah—in full view of two armies, Philistine and Israelite, gathered on either side of the valley—kneeling at the brook, exposed and vulnerable **❞** (page 35).

5. How did this opening to the chapter fire up your imagination? What would you say was your primary emotion as you began to read?

6. What other "snapshots" from Scripture or life have this same exquisite tension even with the awareness that what appears to be about to happen in the situation is very different from what actually happens?

"The same debased imagination that treated Goliath as important treated David as insignificant. The men who were in awe of Goliath were contemptuous of David. Arriving with ten loaves of bread and ten bricks of cheese for his brothers in the army, David was treated by them with withering scorn. Their imaginations were so ruined by Goliath-watching that they were incapable of seeing and accepting a simple act of friendship " (page 39).

7. What was it about "Goliath-watching" that had such a harmful effect on the soldiers of Israel and Saul?

8. What made David's imagination so different?

9. Why was Saul's offer of assistance to David limited by the king's imagination?

" Until David walked into the Valley of Elah and knelt at that brook, the only options seemed to be a bullying Might or a fearful Right. Take your choice: brutal Goliath or anxious Saul.

David kneeling, unhurried and calm, opened up another option: God, God's ways, God's salvation. How do we so easily lose sight of this, lose awareness of God? Why would any of us in our right minds exchange a God-blessed imagination capable of 'seeing the invisible' for a mess of statistics? But however it happens, David kneeling at the brook leads our recovery " (page 44).

10. How many people present that day at Elah decided to take what was behind door number 3?

11. If God had spoken aloud about David that day, what do you think he would have said?

LARGER STORY

" And so it turns out that the David/Goliath story is as important for adults as it ever was for children. One of the great impoverishments of many adult lives is the absence of children's stories, whether read or told or listened to " (page 37).

12. How does Peterson explain this point of importance? What do adults get from the David/Goliath showdown story? (See page 37.)

13. What other stories recorded in the Bible have this quality of capturing the imagination to teach a lesson? Start with the following list and add several, noting the "adult" lesson you see in the story:

- Noah's Ark (Genesis 6–8)
- Crossing the Red Sea (Exodus 14)
- Jonah and the Whale (Jonah)

" The theme of the David story is becoming human. What does it mean to be human, *become* human, be a real woman, a real man? What must we deal with in order to become ourselves, to grow up? " (page 39).

14. What three David episodes does Peterson note as foundational, "a kind of narrative tripod, upon which the rest of the David stories will be built"? (See page 39.)

15. How does developing a God-dominated imagination contribute to someone's becoming a real woman or a real man?

16. In what way does the outline of David's development of a God-dominated imagination point to the kinds of practices anyone can do in becoming alive to God's presence? (See page 40.)

YOUR STORY

" David at that moment, kneeling at the brook, frames something that's absolutely essential for each of us. Are we going to live this life from our knees, imaginatively and personally? Or are we going to live it conventionally and at secondhand? Are we going to live out of our God-created, Spirit-anointed, Jesus-saved being? Or are we going to toady and defer to eunuch professionals? Are we going to be shaped by our fears of Goliath or by God? Are we going to live by our admiration of Saul or by God? " (page 42).

17. There are six questions in the quote you just read. Reread them, taking a moment to write your personal answer to each one:
   a.

   b.

   c.

   d.

e.

f.

18. Which one of those questions comes the closest to confronting the point of tension in your relationship with God today? Why?

19. Peterson ends this chapter with a description of David, on his feet, sprinting toward Goliath, closing with the enemy (see page 44). How do you see the connection between time on your knees and the challenge to run toward the obstacles of life?

20. In what ways do you recognize your need for a more truly "prayer-saturated" and "God-dominated" imagination as you live for God?

FOR PRAYERFUL REFLECTION

Take some time to feed your imagination. Spend some time in a wilderness place; even find a brook where you can kneel. Don't close your eyes, but feast your vision on the evidence of God's creativity and power around you. Let the obstacles and opposition diminish as your mind dwells on God. Ask him for some "smooth stones" you can carry from that place as you run to battle!

FRIENDSHIP

David and Jonathan

READ

1 Samuel 18–20
Chapter 5, pages 47–57

THEME WORD: FRIENDSHIP

"Friending" is one of the new words for our times. Is it possible to describe that process as anything remotely like the flesh-and-blood development of genuine friendship? David's life shows us that real friends come in ones, not stacks. One friend who has your back is worth more than an impressive pile of friends in name only.

    1. When was the last time a friend really came through for you? How have you expressed your gratitude?

KEY PASSAGES

This is the very best way to love. Put your life on the line for your friends. You are my friends when you do the things I command you. (John 15:13-14)

1 Samuel 18–20
Psalm 7
Proverbs 17:17; 18:24; 27:6
Romans 5:1-5

DAVID'S STORY

2. Why would it be somewhat unlikely that David and Jonathan would become friends?

3. How did David know that Jonathan was a true friend?

4. In what ways did Jonathan try to mediate between David and Saul? (See 1 Samuel 19:1-7.)

5. How do you think Jonathan was able to balance his loyalty to David and his loyalty to his father without betraying either?

" David's experience with enmity was one of the powerful shaping influences in his life. Much of his spirituality—the way he prayed, the way he lived—can be accounted for only by understanding the ways he experienced and handled enmity " (page 47).

6. What is enmity?

7. As you think about the process God used in David's life, read Romans 5:1-5 (NIV). In place of the word "suffering" there, substitute "enmity." Does it fit? What was God doing in David's life?

" Jonathan lived out his covenantal friendship with David in hard circumstances. The friendship covenant served God's purposes in David, but Jonathan got little or no emotional reward. Jonathan never saw David again after helping him escape from Saul. Jonathan lived out his covenant of friendship in circumstances that were anti-David. For the rest of his life he served in Saul's court, fighting with his father in the Philistine wars and accompanying him, presumably, on the David hunts. But the circumstances didn't cancel out the covenant; rather, the covenant was used in the purposes of God to overcome the circumstances " (page 53).

8. Cases like Jonathan and David's point out that friendship isn't measured by reciprocal exchanges of affection. One friend may end up owing the other a lot! So what benefit comes to someone like Jonathan, who kept his side of the covenant even though he "got little or no emotional reward" for his faithfulness?

9. In describing the impact of genuine friendship, Peterson says, "Friendship *forms*" (page 53). What does he mean by that expression?

LARGER STORY

" Friendship is a much underestimated aspect of spirituality. It's every bit as significant as prayer and fasting " (page 53).

10. What does Peterson mean and how does his thought apply to Jonathan and David?

11. What evidence can you find in 1 Samuel 18–20 that Jonathan "discerned God in David, comprehended the danger and difficulty of his anointing, and made a covenant of friendship with him" (page 53)?

" Lacking confirmation by the word of a friend, our most promising beginnings fizzle. Lacking confirmation in the presence of a friend, our bravest ventures unravel. It's not unusual for any of us to begin something wonderful, and it's not unusual for any of us to do things that are quite good. But it *is* unusual to continue and to persevere " (page 55).

12. What reasons does Peterson give for this sequence of events?

13. What exactly does the term "confirmation" mean in this description of a friend's role? (See also page 57.)

YOUR STORY

" Evil doesn't stand a chance against goodness. Persecution is futile in the presence of faithfulness. Hostility is picayune compared to friendship.

This isn't the view that's current among us. Politically and psychologically we operate from a different set of assumptions, and as a consequence we spend enormous sums of money and expend tremendous energy on defense. But if we're to live largely and freely in the context of God, we must learn what God has revealed to us " (page 56).

14. As you think about the expectations and shortcomings of friendships around you, how would you describe our "different set of assumptions" mentioned above?

15. What has God "revealed to us" in this chapter of David's story?

16. How have you experienced the amazing power of a confirming friendship? When was the last time you applied that confirming power in one of your friendships?

FOR PRAYERFUL REFLECTION

Choose a couple of friends you value and spend some deliberate time thoughtfully praying for them. Ask God to help you see how you could offer them a confirming word or action. Pray out of your understanding of their character and their lives. Take time to write out what you've prayed and give it to them, not necessarily with explanation.

SANCTUARY

David and Doeg

READ
1 Samuel 21–22
Chapter 6, pages 59–69

THEME WORD: SANCTUARY
We know that birds benefit from sanctuary, and wildlife flourishes in a refuge, but do we need that kind of protection? What does sanctuary do for us? Is it a place to escape from the enemy, or a place to meet God?

1. What are the three places you most often use to find sanctuary?

KEY PASSAGES

GOD, *my shepherd!*
  I don't need a thing.
You have bedded me down in lush meadows,
    you find me quiet pools to drink from.
True to your word,
    you let me catch my breath
      and send me in the right direction. (Psalm 23:1-3)

Leviticus 24:5-9
1 Samuel 21–22
Psalm 52
Matthew 12:1-5
Hebrews 10:31; 12:25-29

DAVID'S STORY

2. How did Ahimelech react when David showed up on his door-step, and what might have been his reasons? (See 1 Samuel 21:1-9.)

3. Despite his reservations, how did Ahimelech help David?

4. Two men visited Nob for different purposes: David and Doeg. How is the character of these two men held in sharp contrast in the story?

5. When Doeg directed Saul's anger toward Ahimelech, how did the priest respond with integrity? (See 1 Samuel 22:6-15.)

❝ David is well launched by now into a life of holiness—a life defined and initiated by God. But he's also being assaulted by its opposite. He runs to Ahimelech's sanctuary at Nob for protection, and then he finds himself immersed in holiness. A sanctuary is a place for paying attention to God, a place where the truth of God is preserved and honored, a place for remembering the events in which God has been clearly active and powerful **❞** (page 61).

6. How does God meet David's needs at Nob? What kind of sanctuary does he find?

7. What rules does Ahimelech bend in order to keep deeper rules and help David?

❝ This is perhaps the place to note that the story of David isn't set before us as a moral model to copy. David isn't a person whose actions we're inspired to imitate. In the company of David we don't feel inadequate because we know we could never do it that well. Just the opposite: in the company of David we find someone who does it as badly as, or worse than, we do, but who in the process doesn't quit, doesn't withdraw from God. David's isn't an *ideal* life but an *actual* life **❞** (page 62).

8. In what senses would it be appropriate to call David's life one of holy perseverance?

9. So, if David is not a "moral model to copy," then what are the benefits of following him through these events in his life?

" Ahimelech and David had different ideas of what the sanctuary was for that day, but David's approach prevailed. And Ahimelech *let* it prevail. He was hesitant, not quite sure of what was going on, but he didn't stand in the way " (page 64).

10. Why do you think it was important that Ahimelech let David's use of the sanctuary prevail that day?

LARGER STORY

" I want to use the word *sanctuary* to represent all holy places and not restrict it to shrines and temples, cathedrals and chapels. A holy place is where we become aware that there's more to life than meets the eye, and that the more is 'other.' *Other*. God, who is beyond us, is also at hand " (page 64).

11. What is the range of holy places, sanctuaries, that Peterson finds in Scripture and in the world?

12. What are the two parallel purposes for sanctuaries, and why must both be fulfilled from time to time? (See pages 64–65.)

“ For a man like Doeg, a sanctuary isn't a place to seek an intensification of everyday life but a place to acquire a patina of self-righteousness that will give some holy polish to everyday life. A sanctuary, for someone like Doeg, isn't a place to expose weakness but a place to acquire a cover ” (page 66).

13. How do Doeg's presence at Nob and his actions afterward illustrate the limitations of sanctuary?

14. Saul and Doeg had the same basic understanding of sanctuary, but how did that understanding cut them off from ever finding real sanctuary?

YOUR STORY

" One of the distressing and distressingly frequent corruptions that works its way into the spiritual life is the loss of connection between who God is and who we are. We say the name *God*, we enter a sanctuary, we pray—but often the slightest tone of falsehood begins to creep in, a subtle dishonesty that gets into our speech and our action; the religious place offers an occasion to *use* God instead of submitting to him. Instead of becoming *more* before God, we become *less*. David is an antidote to this. We read David to cultivate a sense of reality for a true life, an honest life, a God-aware life and God-responsive life **"** (page 62).

15. How has this time dwelling on the life of David affected your awareness of life and of God?

16. What experiences have you had in your relationship with God of the "corruption" of honesty that Peterson describes?

" The spirituality of sanctuary is fundamental to the Christian life. We need sanctuaries to run to in order to sustain ourselves with what is necessary to live—God and God's provisions for living in a dangerous world that's hostile to faith. Holy places are necessary for holy living **"** (page 65).

17. What are the current holy places in your life, and what do you find there? (See page 69.)

18. In what way would you describe your current condition as holy living?

FOR PRAYERFUL REFLECTION

In the sense described by Peterson, what holy places do you have in your life that wouldn't be seen as that by anyone else? The mundane has become holy because God has met you there. What do you think would happen if you made your visits to those places more of a habit?

WILDERNESS

David at En-gedi

READ

1 Samuel 23–24

Chapter 7, pages 71–80

THEME WORD: WILDERNESS

The "wild" in wilderness is what gets our attention. Untamed, unexpected, and dangerous—we enjoy thinking we could handle places like that, as long as they didn't actually live up to their billing. Pristine wilderness is the stuff of photographs, not what you experience when you are there, surrounded and immersed in elements that are mesmerizing, uncontrollable, and deeply humbling.

KEY PASSAGES

At once, this same Spirit pushed Jesus out into the wild. For forty wilderness days and nights he was tested by Satan. Wild animals were his companions, and angels took care of him. (Mark 1:12-13)

1 Samuel 23–24

DAVID'S STORY

1. Why did David go to Keilah? (See 1 Samuel 23:1-13.)

2. Who encouraged David in the wilderness? (See 1 Samuel 23:14-18.)

3. What was the state of mind of Saul when David spared his life in the wilderness? (See 1 Samuel 24:8-21.)

66 David didn't start out in the wilderness, and he didn't end up in the wilderness. But he did spend some highly significant years in the wilderness. Everybody—at least everybody who has anything to do with God—spends time in the wilderness, so it's important to know what can take place there 99 (page 72).

4. What *can* take place in the wilderness?

5. Peterson mentions two other significant figures—Moses (Exodus) and Jesus (Matthew 4:1-11)—who spent formative time in the wilderness. How would you compare the experiences of these three? How was each experience different?

❝ In the wilderness years, as David was dealing with God, a sense of the sacred developed in him. While he was living in that austere country, his awareness of holiness, of God's beauty and presence in everything, in everyone, increased exponentially. David was above all reverent. He had an inordinate capacity for wonder. The Psalms, many of which came out of these wilderness years, are our main evidence for this. This story puts the holiness on display ❞ (page 77).

6. How does David's response when he had Saul in a terribly vulnerable position in the cave give evidence of his "sense of the sacred"?

7. In what ways did David also find holiness and refuge in the wilderness? (See page 78.)

8. What is your favorite psalm? Does it give any evidence of having been written in the wilderness, or with the wilderness in mind? How?

LARGER STORY

❝ In the wilderness we're face to face with the basics, the Basic, with God. The confrontation is a test, a temptation. Do we deal with God or not? We take the test and become more or less. We grow up or we regress. David became more. David grew up.

And so we read these David stories of the wilderness years and look for signs of God, look for evidence of David's God-responses. It's good practice for discovering similar God-responses in the wilderness circumstances of our own lives and the lives of our friends ❞ (page 76).

9. What are the signs of a wilderness experience in someone's life? What are some ways that we create wilderness (not necessarily the beneficial kind) in our own lives?

10. What is it about wilderness experiences of any kind that make them good training ground for God-responses (even watching others go through them)?

66 A thousand years before St. Paul wrote that our bodies are temples of the Holy Spirit—holy *places*—David had discovered and experienced this fundamental truth in the unlikely body of King Saul in the wilderness of En-gedi 99 (page 78).

11. Peterson is referring to Paul's words to the Corinthians when he wrote, "Or didn't you realize that your body is a sacred place, the place of the Holy Spirit? Don't you see that you can't live however you please, squandering what God paid such a high price for? The physical part of you is not some piece of property belonging to the spiritual part of you" (1 Corinthians 6:19). How was David recognizing the Holy Spirit's special relationship with Saul?

12. Even though, as 1 Samuel 16:14 tells us, "At that very moment the Spirit of GOD left Saul and in its place a black mood sent by GOD settled on him. He was terrified," David was still honoring the special role God had called Saul to fulfill, though Saul had failed. God may have relieved Saul of duty, but did God reject Saul? Why or why not?

YOUR STORY
13. Where in your life right now might there be some places that should be labeled wilderness on your life map? Why?

14. What are you learning in those places? How is God meeting you there?

" This happens all the time; it's one of the fundamental surprises in spirituality. Whatever we start out feeling or doing or thinking can lead us to God, whether directly or meanderingly. Another way to say this is that we rarely start with God. We start with the immediate data of our lives—a messy house, a balky car, a cranky spouse, a recalcitrant child (and on our good days a burst of sunshine, an ecstatic smile, a piercing insight). We start out being desperate in the wilderness of En-gedi, and before we know it we're ecstatic in the wilderness of God **"** (page 79).

15. So, do you want to revise your "personal wilderness list" on page 59? Do it now, while it's fresh on your mind.

16. When was the last time you started out in the wilderness and ended up in God's presence? What difference did that encounter make in you?

FOR PRAYERFUL REFLECTION

Wilderness is for getting along with less, for sharpening our wits, for altering our priorities, for, as Peterson puts it, getting down to "the Basic, with God." One of David's recurring strategies was to find a point of worship or gratitude as the first step out of a wilderness moment. Find a point of worship or gratitude today, and meet God there—and see where that leads.

BEAUTY

David and Abigail

READ

1 Samuel 25

Chapter 8, pages 81–89

THEME WORD: BEAUTY

Is beauty just in the eye of the beholder, or does beauty touch the heart in ways that are hard to express? Does beauty hurt? Does it heal? Is it really only skin deep, or is beauty so much more than skin deep? David certainly discovered the disarming grace that true beauty wields.

KEY PASSAGES

The Word became flesh and blood,
*   and moved into the neighborhood.*
We saw the glory with our own eyes,
*   the one-of-a-kind glory,*
*   like Father, like Son,*
Generous inside and out,
*   true from start to finish. (John 1:14)*

1 Samuel 25

Psalm 14

DAVID'S STORY

1. What significant note is included in the first verse of
1 Samuel 25 that must have affected David? Why?

2. Before Abigail intervened, what other unnamed person spoke
with integrity and set in motion the events that saved the day?

" Abigail on her knees in the wilderness, on her knees before David.
David is rampaging, murder in his eyes, and Abigail blocks his path,
kneeling before him. David has been insulted and is out to avenge the
insult with four hundred men worked up into a frenzy. Abigail, soli-
tary and beautiful, kneels in the path, stopping David in his tracks. At
this moment David is full of himself and empty of God; the emptiness
is visible as ugliness. Abigail recovers God for David. David is earlier
described as beautiful, though there's no sign of it here. But beautiful
Abigail restores the beauty of God to David, his original identity **"**
(page 82).

3. What made David stop? What was it about that encounter that
you think got David's attention?

4. Given the original offense on the part of Nabal, how could
David have responded differently? According to the timing in

1 Samuel 25:14-17, what might have happened if David had waited longer to demand satisfaction?

" Abigail says, in effect, 'Your task, David, is not to exact vengeance; vengeance is God's business, and you aren't God. You're out here in the wilderness to find out what God is doing and who you are before God. The wilderness isn't an experiment station in which you test yourself and find out how strong and resilient you are. It's where you discover the strength of God and God's faithful ways of working in and through your life. Nabal is a fool, but don't you become a fool. One fool is enough in this story **"** (page 85).

5. What would have made David a fool? After all, wasn't he simply righting a wrong, confronting an injustice?

6. At this point in the story, what role did Abigail play in David's life?

LARGER STORY

" When some Abigail or other shows up—a sudden beauty in song or face, in aspen or iris—we see ourselves in a larger, truer light. David had been living in the huge, vast world of God—God's love and redemption, prayer and holiness—and it nearly got away from him as he pursued his puny, small-minded revenge. Abigail's beauty—her double-edged beauty of character and countenance—recovered the beauty of the Lord for him. Abigail on her knees put David back on his knees " (page 88).

7. What are some other examples of compelling beauty that can knock us out of the saddle when we're headed in the wrong direction?

8. What does it mean to "see ourselves in a larger, truer light"? When that happens, what do we do?

" There's a long tradition in the Christian life, most developed in Eastern Orthodoxy, of honoring beauty as a witness to God and a call to prayer. Beauty is never only what our senses report to us but always also a sign of what's just beyond our senses—an innerness and depth " (page 85).

9. How does beauty get distorted in an evil world? How is it twisted or devalued?

10. Given the general inability of the world (and sometimes our own inability) to recognize beauty as a pointer toward God, what would be some ways we might reclaim, if only in our own responses, a God-responsive sensitivity to beauty?

YOUR STORY

"There's nothing more common in the spiritual life than starting out right and then going wrong " (page 88).

11. How would you illustrate the truth of this observation from your own life?

12. Peterson mentions Paul's use of the term *shipwreck* in 1 Timothy 1:19: "By rejecting this, some have made shipwreck of their faith" (ESV). What disciplines, habits, and actions are you building into your voyage in life to prevent ending up a shipwreck?

13. What beautiful things are you aware of in your life right now that have prevented you from making terrible mistakes? How did those beautiful things get where they are?

FOR PRAYERFUL REFLECTION

Evil cannot create beauty; it can only distort, deface, and destroy beauty. Take some time to contemplate something or someone beautiful in your life. Thank God for the privilege of having that beauty.

COMPANY

David at Ziklag

READ
1 Samuel 27
Chapter 9, pages 91–101

THEME WORD: COMPANY

Misery loves company. What does that mean? Does misery love more misery? Or do people experiencing misery take comfort in the company of others who are miserable? Do we have to be miserable in order for the miserable to love our company? Or is there a kind of indescribable esprit de corps that arises when people face misery together?

1. What kind of company do you keep? What kind of company are you?

KEY PASSAGES

Later Jesus and his disciples were at home having supper with a collection of disreputable guests. Unlikely as it seems, more than a few of them had become followers. The religion scholars and Pharisees saw him keeping this kind of company and lit into his disciples: "What kind of example is this, acting cozy with the riffraff?"

Jesus, overhearing, shot back, "Who needs a doctor: the healthy or the sick? I'm here inviting the sin-sick, not the spiritually-fit."
(Mark 2:15-17)

1 Samuel 21:10-15; 22:1-2; 27
Psalm 55; 133

DAVID'S STORY

2. According to 1 Samuel 22:1-2, why did people flock to David while he was on the run in the wilderness? After reading the key passage from Mark, how were Jesus and David's followers similar?

3. In 1 Samuel 27:1-4, Saul discovered that David was in Gath. Why did Saul stop trying to kill David?

4. Who did David take with him when he moved to Gath and why did those people go with him?

" A completely unexpected and most improbable 'best' that occurred in David's wilderness years was the formation of a people of God—a community of the sort that we now call a church. As usual, though,

we're dealing not with a generalized 'best' but with something particular, something with its own personal name. Adullam to begin with,
and then Ziklag **"** (page 93).

5. What is it about camaraderie or company that would lead a
group under certain circumstances to take on church-like character? What happens in a church that for one reason or another
becomes a company of the committed?

6. Does God still work in places where he is not directly recognized? Why and how does God do that?

" These are the people David lived with for that decade of wilderness
years. They foraged together, ate together, prayed together, fought
together. There's nothing explicit in the text about the spirituality of
David's company—nothing that says they became a community of
faith and searched out the ways in which God worked his salvation in
their lives—but the context demands it **"** (pages 94–95).

7. What is it about the context and the participants that demand
some inclusion of God in the picture? How might David and
Abiathar the priest have had something to do with calling the
company toward attention to God?

8. David's company of fighting men and their families ended up in Philistine country, pretending to be allies of King Achish. Peterson points out that the gift of Ziklag to David's band is handled either from a moralizing or a secularizing perspective. What do those two terms mean? (See pages 97–98.)

9. What other, often overlooked, explanation for the meaning of Ziklag puts God right in the middle of things? (See page 98.)

LARGER STORY

" The storyteller doesn't say that this [David's time and actions while at Ziklag] is the right thing to do, simply that this is what David does. And in precisely these conditions, God works out his purposes. God protects David from violating the covenant; he guards David's faithfulness to his anointing; he works out his salvation. The primary concern of the spiritual life isn't what we do for God but what God does for us " (pages 98–99).

10. So, what do we take away as a general lesson from David's immersion in the life of cultural values so foreign to his own, particularly concerning God?

11. Rephrase the closing sentence from the quote on page 72 in your own words. How would you state the details of the "primary concern"?

66 I know scores of men and women who are living under the patronage of Achish of Gath. . . .

And what I want to say is this: God is perfectly capable of working out his purposes in our lives even when we can't lift a finger to help. Better yet, God is faithfully working out our salvation even when every time we lift a finger it seems to contribute to the wrong side, the Philistine side 99 (page 99).

12. How do we persevere when we find ourselves in circumstances that are out of our control? If God is in control, what is our part?

13. When we look at verses like Romans 8:28, what should be our expectations when it comes to aiming at a perfect situation where we can live for God? Where do we get the idea that such a place even exists?

YOUR STORY

" Ziklag, for me, is the premier biblical location for realizing that when we get serious about the Christian life we eventually end up in a place and among people decidedly uncongenial to what we had expected. That place and people is often called a church. It's hard to get over the disappointment that God, having made an exception in my case, doesn't call nice people to repentance " (page 100).

14. Based on this chapter, how would you describe Peterson's understanding of the church? How closely does the description fit your church?

15. Where and how do you fit in that church? What does fitting have to do with anything if that's the place God has called you to be?

" Disillusioned, we go off on our own and cultivate a pure spirituality uncontaminated by religious hucksters and hypocrites. But eventually, if we're honest and reading our Bibles honestly, we find we can't do it. We can't survive in the wilderness alone. We need others, and we need a leader. And then we begin to get it: God's purposes are being worked out most profoundly when we're least aware of them " (page 100).

16. In what ways can you identify with some aspect of what
Peterson has noted?

17. What happens when we try to survive in the wilderness alone?

FOR PRAYERFUL REFLECTION

Read the following passage of Scripture prayerfully, seeking to identify
with both individuals represented in Jesus' story:

> He told his next story to some who were complacently pleased with
> themselves over their moral performance and looked down their
> noses at the common people: "Two men went up to the Temple to
> pray, one a Pharisee, the other a tax man. The Pharisee posed and
> prayed like this: 'Oh, God, I thank you that I am not like other
> people—robbers, crooks, adulterers, or, heaven forbid, like this tax
> man. I fast twice a week and tithe on all my income.'
>
> "Meanwhile the tax man, slumped in the shadows, his face in
> his hands, not daring to look up, said, 'God, give mercy. Forgive
> me, a sinner.'"
>
> Jesus commented, "This tax man, not the other, went home
> made right with God." (Luke 18:9-14)

CHAPTER 10

GENEROSITY

David at the Brook Besor

READ
1 Samuel 30
Chapter 10, pages 103–112

THEME WORD: GENEROSITY
Fairness is frequently a one-way street: *I definitely believe you should be fair with me; the necessity for me to be fair with you is up for discussion.* Generosity is often decidedly unfair. It offers to someone what he or she hasn't earned or doesn't deserve. Salvation is the immeasurable and shockingly unfair gift of generosity from God: "He saved us, not because of righteous things we had done, but because of his mercy. He saved us through the washing of rebirth and renewal by the Holy Spirit, whom he poured out on us generously through Jesus Christ our Savior" (Titus 3:5-6, NIV). Every other act of genuine generosity has that same shocking flavor.

1. What person comes to mind when you think of generosity?

KEY PASSAGES

Then those "sheep" are going to say, "Master, what are you talking about? When did we ever see you hungry and feed you, thirsty and give you a drink? And when did we ever see you sick or in prison and come to you?" Then the King will say, "I'm telling the solemn truth: Whenever you did one of these things to someone overlooked or ignored, that was me—you did it to me." (Matthew 25:37-40)

1 Samuel 30
Psalm 36
Matthew 11:28-30

DAVID'S STORY

2. In the sequence of events in this episode, what was the first thing David did when he and his men realized they had lost everything?

3. How do you think the answer David got from God influenced everything else that happened as this episode unfolded?

4. After reading this account, how would you respond to Peterson's efforts to put the Brook Besor as one of the highlights in David's story?

" Catastrophe brings out either the best or the worst in us. At Ziklag it first brought out the worst. . . . Spiritual formation is a slow business. And then this Amalekite disaster wiped out not only their homes and families but every bit of slowly acquired righteousness as well **"** (page 105).

> 5. What was the "worst" that showed up several times in this story?

> 6. In what sense is spiritual formation a slow business?

" But there were mean-spirited men among the four hundred, who bristled at the notion of sharing the victory booty with their weaker brothers. It was enough that they get their wives and children back, but nothing else—not a single piece of Amalekite plunder, not so much as one sheep or goat or heifer **"** (page 109).

> 7. How does the response of the four hundred mirror what you would describe as typical human behavior?

> 8. What practical reasons can you think of that would explain the group staying behind at the brook as a wise tactic for the entire effort to retrieve the lost families and possessions?

" Everything they experienced was sheer grace. How could they talk about dividing things up fairly? God was treating them with marvelous and generous grace; David would see to it that they treated one another with marvelous and generous grace **"** (page 110).

9. How would you describe David's actions and responses from the time that his men turned on him when they first discovered Ziklag had been sacked?

10. How was David's decision to share the booty equally an example of his practice of gracious leadership?

LARGER STORY

" There's an enormous amount of outrage in the world that's converted into angry plans of attack and destruction. A great deal of social action and political reform is fueled by anger; the results are nearly always worse than the conditions that provoked the action **"** (page 105).

11. What examples of this observation can you identify in the goings-on around you in society today?

12. How does Peterson's answer to this problem, derived from David's example, resonate with you? (See page 106.)

" The Brook Besor is narrative nutrition: a story that feeds an essential aspect of our God-designed humanity. In a world of disembodied advice it puts our size-seven bone-and-flesh feet on dirt and rock ground. I want to pull the Brook Besor from its undeserved obscurity and put it on our maps—*name* what we might otherwise miss because we had filed it under some category such as 'care,' or 'charity,' or 'generosity' **"** (page 104).

13. What subtitle would you give the Brook Besor to highlight its unique role in David's spiritual formation? How would "Sweet Victory of Unfairness" fit?

" But we live in an age that has replaced compassion with sentiment. Sentiment is a feeling disconnected from relationship. Sentiment is *spilled* compassion. It looks like concern; it could develop into compassion, but it never does. . . .

One of the supreme ironies of our age is that the society that has talked and written most about the fulfillment of the self shows the least evidence of it. People obsessed with the cultivation of the self have nothing to show for it but a cult of selfishness. A few generations of economic affluence, political liberation, and religious freedom have flowered into obesity, anxiety, and meanness **"** (pages 110–111).

14. What examples of unexpected (and from the world's view, unfair) generosity have you observed?

15. By loudly proclaiming as a culture that we're trying to make things fair for everyone, how have we ended up depriving people of the responsibility and opportunity to be generous, to be deliberately "unfair" with others who do nothing to deserve it?

YOUR STORY

66 One of the reasons that Christians are dispersed in the world is to recover a life for others and practice a priesthood of all believers—connect with others in an earthy, Davidic compassion so thoroughly that no expert or professional can ever again bluff us into passivity or consumerism 99 (page 111).

16. What kind of personal responsibility does a statement like this engender in your life? Where have you had to make the choice to be generous?

17. How do you resolve the internal sense that generosity violates fairness? When have you benefited from someone else's personal, costly generosity?

FOR PRAYERFUL REFLECTION

Take some time to think about the unfairness of God's grace in your life. Recognize that God finds you at the Brook Besor and nowhere else that would indicate you have anything to contribute to what God does. Ask God to help you become so overwhelmed by his generosity that you can't help but be more generous to others.

CHAPTER 11

GRIEF

David in Lament

READ

2 Samuel 1

Chapter 11, pages 113–121

THEME WORD: GRIEF

The world has an answer for grief: it's *closure*. No sooner does tragedy strike or loss devastate, than someone nods wisely and speaks of closure. The crushing weight and reality of a painful occurrence becomes a news sound bite that must be wrapped up quickly, so the shallow and uncaring words of closure pretend to sound like compassion. Grief has its own language, its own timing, and its own agenda, and if our primary intent is to "get it behind us" we will miss the depth of healing that grief can allow us to experience.

1. What does grief mean in your life?

KEY PASSAGES

When Jesus saw her sobbing and the Jews with her sobbing, a deep anger welled up within him. He said, "Where did you put him?"

85

"Master, come and see," they said. Now Jesus wept.
The Jews said, "Look how deeply he loved him." (John 11:33-36)

1 Samuel 31
2 Samuel 1

DAVID'S STORY

2. First Samuel 31 gives the final chapter of Saul and Jonathan's lives. Where do you see both tragedy and triumph in that chapter?

3. Second Samuel 1:11-12 describes how David and his men responded when they got the news of Saul's death. How would you explain this behavior as part of the whole story? Why do you think David's men responded the way he did?

❝ But if my Aunt Frieda accommodated my childhood imagination to the legitimacy and pervasiveness of grief, David trained my adult spirituality in grief rightly grieved. David's mighty lament over the deaths of Saul and Jonathan draws us into the depths of a healthy human spirit as it deals honestly and prayerfully with devastating loss and all its attendant emotions ❞ (page 115).

4. When you read David's lament in 2 Samuel 1:19-27, what gives those phrases their texture and depth? Why did David want his lament taught to the people? (See page 119.)

5. How is the difference in relationship between David and Saul and between David and Jonathan expressed in the lament?

" It seems odd, even contradictory, that in order to live totally we must face death totally. But it's true. David, who lived exuberantly, also lamented fiercely. His exuberance and lamentations were aspects of the same life-orientation and commitment: life *matters*. David honored human life—the sheer fact of human life—extravagantly. The depth of the lamentation witnesses the extent of the veneration " (page 115).

6. Why does facing death totally allow us the capacity to live totally?

7. How does David also demonstrate this defenseless ability to enter into grief later in 2 Samuel 12:15-23? Where did God fit into the experience of grief for David?

LARGER STORY

" David lamented because he cared. David lamented because he was willing and able to bring his total attention to the fact of death. Because David lamented with this lamentation recorded in 2 Samuel 1, we have access to an aspect of experience that's absolutely essential if we're going to live God-responsively, live God-abundantly **"** (page 115).

8. What is so crucial about developing the ability to give total attention to the fact of death?

9. What does the typical response to death that you've observed tell you about the spiritual condition of the society in which you live?

" There's no lament because truth isn't taken seriously, love isn't taken seriously. Human life doesn't matter as *life*—God-given, Christ-redeemed, Spirit-blessed life. It counts only as 'news.' There's no dignity to any of it. It's trivialized **"** (page 116).

10. How is the process of grief an opportunity to express both truth and love? In what ways?

11. Have you noticed an almost unremarked longing in people for some way to express laments? Often news stories, particularly of violent deaths by accident or murder, are followed by scenes of people placing flowers, cards, and even visiting the sites of the tragedies. Is this grief or something else?

12. What is a healthy way to respond to the death of strangers?

YOUR STORY

" Death isn't the worst thing. The worst thing is failing to deal with reality and becoming disconnected from what is actual. The worst thing is trivializing the honorable, desecrating the sacred. What I do with my grief affects the way you handle your grief; together we form a community that deals with death and other loss in the context of God's sovereignty, which is expressed finally in resurrection " (page 120).

13. Who has been your "Aunt Frieda" and taught you about grief and death? How have they done that?

14. Because grief is inevitable, what has been your way of responding to these experiences? Has this chapter confirmed or challenged the way you face death? In what ways?

" We don't become mature human beings by getting lucky or cleverly circumventing loss, and certainly not by avoidance and distraction. Learn to lament. Learn *this* lamentation. We're *mortals*, after all. We and everyone around are scheduled for death (*mortis*). Get used to it. Take up your cross. It prepares us and those around us for resurrection " (page 121).

15. What would someone conclude about your view of God's sovereignty and your confidence in the resurrection by the way you grieve?

16. Are there some recent losses that you need to revisit with a lament because you know you've been distracted from the truth that's there? What will you do?

FOR PRAYERFUL REFLECTION

Read over David's lament again (2 Samuel 1:19-27). With its words fresh in your mind, ask God if there is someone in your life who has gone unlamented. Give God enough time to break your heart with the weight of a loss of something so immeasurably valued to him as a life.

BONEHEADS

David and the Sons of Zeruiah

READ

2 Samuel 2–4

Chapter 12, pages 123–130

THEME WORD: BONEHEADS

Boneheads are hardheads. And boneheads often result in hard hearts. With boneheads, what you see is what you get. Boneheads usually mean a kind of consistency that can exhibit great loyalty or unyielding enmity. What boneheads find most difficult to do is change or alter behavior. Boneheads can bring joy in single-mindedness, but they most often are the cause of sorrow.

KEY PASSAGES

James and John, Zebedee's sons, came up to him. "Teacher, we have something we want you to do for us. . . . Arrange it," they said, "so that we will be awarded the highest places of honor in your glory—one of us at your right, the other at your left." . . .

Jesus got them together to settle things down. "You've observed how godless rulers throw their weight around," he said, "and when people get a little power how quickly it goes to their heads. It's not going

to be that way with you. Whoever wants to be great must become a
servant." (Mark 10:35,37,42-43)

2 Samuel 2–4
1 Kings 2:31

DAVID'S STORY

1. What are your own impressions of Joab and his brothers from
those three chapters in 2 Samuel? How would having them as
allies be a mixed blessing?

2. How does the episode in 2 Samuel 18:5-17 give you a glimpse
into Joab's true priorities?

3. Second Samuel 2:18-28 describes the death of Asahel at the
hand of Abner. How does this event represent the character of the
sons of Zeruiah?

" David, after a decade of being hunted down in the wilderness, living
on the defensive, is now in a position of strength. He's thirty years
old, and the *ruler*. The tables have turned. He's no longer running,
hiding, living by his wits. He's in charge. He's operating now from a
position of authority. What kind of strength will he use? How will he
exercise his authority? " (page 125).

4. As the new king, what lessons did David bring with him from the wilderness? How did they affect the way he ruled?

5. Why is a sudden change of fortune in one direction or another so difficult for a person to absorb? What does David show us about assuming power?

" In the footnotes we still detect David at his characteristic kingwork: acting generously (with Jabesh-gilead, 2 Sam. 2:5-7), raising a family (2 Sam. 3:2-5), enacting a covenant (2 Sam. 3:12-16), writing poetry, and grieving honestly (2 Sam. 3:31-37) " (page 128).

6. What are some of the basic life-habits that a person should maintain no matter what his or her current circumstance in life? Was David's "kingwork" a reflection of his character or of his new position?

" After Joab and Abishai murder Abner, David cries out, 'I am this day weak, though anointed king; these men the sons of Zeruiah are too hard for me' (2 Sam. 3:39 [RSV]). These two sons of Zeruiah are terrific fighting men and fiercely loyal to David's political interests. But Joab and Abishai comprehend nothing of David's spirit; they hate peace and the things that have to do with peace. They want mastery and influence and power " (page 130).

7. What is most frustrating at the personal level about dealing with boneheads? We know how David felt, but how did he deal with these men? (See 1 Kings 2:5-6.)

8. In what ways did David suffer as part of the reality of having men like the sons of Zeruiah in his life?

LARGER STORY

66 It helps, I think, to know that this is a thoroughly biblical situation, very Davidic. When we're learning to read our lives as a gospel story, there's no place or company free from the sons of Zeruiah. It helps to know that the good news has been worked out since time began in exactly these circumstances. It helps to know that the sons of Zeruiah are accounted for in God's economy, and that however difficult they make the life of faith in Jesus, they can't destroy it 99 (pages 124–125).

9. Is there anyone whose life wouldn't fit somewhere as a parallel to the stories in the Bible? What does this tell you about Scripture?

10. Jesus called two of his disciples, James and John, the sons of thunder (sounds a little like "sons of Zeruiah"). What do the character of these men and the outcome of their lives tell you about what might have happened with the sons of Zeruiah if they had actually met David's God?

" We read page after page of this kind of thing and think, What's this doing in the Bible? I don't want to read about jerks like Abner and Joab. I get enough of their kind in the newspapers and on television. I want *good* news. I want the David story. I want to read about Jesus. What the Bible needs is a good editor. Why waste good gospel ink on Abner and Joab? **"** (page 128).

11. Why does God insist on including more than we like of the bad and ugly in what we have come to call "the Good Book"?

12. When we start picking and choosing the contents in the Bible for ourselves do we end up with something better or something worse? Why?

YOUR STORY

" The sons of Zeruiah are in the story; there's no getting around it. . . . That's why so many people quit reading the Bible, or repudiate it: 'I can't read the Bible, especially the Old Testament—too much fighting, too much brutality.' But that's exactly why Christians *do* read it: we find God's purposes being worked out in the precise moral and political, social and cultural conditions that we wake up to each morning, a world of shabby morality and opportunist companions, religious violence, religious propaganda—the many, many sons of Zeruiah that are too hard for us " (page 130).

13. What are your three most personally compelling reasons for reading the Bible?

14. How do you know you're not a son of Zeruiah?

FOR PRAYERFUL REFLECTION

That last question may trouble or even offend you. Think again. The real question isn't the one on the page but the question God would put to you about your responses to him. Take some time to ponder this prayer: "Lord, show me the boneheaded places in my life that I don't see and let my heart and mind be responsive to you."

GROWTH

David and Jerusalem

READ

2 Samuel 5

Chapter 13, pages 131–141

THEME WORD: GROWTH

Growth doesn't always happen when we take over new ground; it often happens when we take over part of a larger ground that contains small strongholds of resistance. The real victories in life are not the external successes but the internal conquests that God makes in the unruly territory of our hearts and lives.

1. As you've immersed yourself in David's story, how have you sensed God's laying siege to strongholds in your life?

KEY PASSAGES

In a word, what I'm saying is, Grow up. *You're kingdom subjects. Now live like it. Live out your God-created identity. Live generously and graciously toward others, the way God lives toward you.* (Matthew 5:48)

Genesis 14:17-24; 27:1; 32:31
2 Samuel 5
Psalm 23

DAVID'S STORY

2. How did the extrabiblical traditions about the taking of Jerusalem broaden your understanding of the special place the city holds even today?

3. Look at Abram's visit with Melchizedek, king of Salem, in Genesis 14:17-24 and David's choice of Jerusalem as his capital here in 2 Samuel 5. In what ways does God's hand seem to be present, moving behind the scenes?

“ In wrapping up the story of the capture of Jerusalem and its establishment as the City of David, 2 Samuel offers this wonderful phrase: 'And David became greater and greater, for the LORD, the God of hosts, was with him' (2 Sam. 5:10 [RSV]). Another way to translate the Hebrew phrase *halok v'gadol* is that David proceeded from that moment with 'a longer stride and a larger embrace' **”** (page 135).

4. How did David lengthen his stride and enlarge his embrace on God as well as on the people over whom he had anointed responsibilities?

5. How does Peterson use this Hebrew phrase to develop the idea of "organic spirituality"? (See pages 137–139.)

" The rise of David is now concluded; the reign of David begins. The words that are used at this inauguration are significant: 'You shall be shepherd of my people Israel, and you shall be prince over Israel' (2 Sam. 5:2 [RSV]). The designation *king* is used freely enough throughout the narrative, but it's not used here: the choice of the words *shepherd* and *prince* is significant **"** (page 139).

6. What is the significance of each of these words in that context: *shepherd* and *prince*?

7. How do these words still affect the story of David as it touches our lives?

" It's impossible to understand a single thing about David apart from God. Every image of this psalm [Psalm 23]—which is to say, every aspect of David's life—is God-defined, God-saturated. Everything that David knows about God he experiences—enters into, embraces, takes into himself **"** (page 141).

8. Now that the shepherd boy of Bethlehem becomes the shepherd king of Israel, how would you describe his relationship with God?

9. How would you explain Psalm 23 as an example of a life-message? How is it a summary statement of everything David understands about God?

LARGER STORY

66 The David story keeps us in touch with our humanity—all of which has to do with God. There's no part of our humanity that isn't God-created and God-conditioned. The David story is a primary way in which the Holy Spirit keeps us in touch, alert and responsive to the gravity and ground of our lives in God the Father, Son, and Holy Spirit and alert to the reality of evil that would destroy or weaken our humanity 99 (page 138).

10. What parts of humanity do you find most compelling in the David story?

11. What, according to Peterson, is the powerful relationship between the David story and the final form of story that comes to us in Jesus Christ? (See page 138.)

" This is why the David story continues to prove so useful: it doesn't show us how we *should* live but how we *do* live **"** (page 139).

12. How do you understand and relate to that statement?

YOUR STORY

13. Glancing up at that last quote again, how have you used the David story more as a set of lenses than a set of lessons?

" When we grow, in contrast to merely change, we venture into new territory and include more people in our lives—serve more and love more. Our culture is filled with change; it's poor in growth. New things, models, developments, opportunities are announced, breathlessly, every hour. But instead of becoming ingredients in a long and wise growth, they simply replace **"** (page 136).

14. Using the statement above as a starting point, how would you define growth in your life?

15. What are some opportunities or offers in your life right now that have more to do with change and little to do with growth? How are you handling them?

FOR PRAYERFUL REFLECTION

The Twenty-Third Psalm is short on task and long on basking in God's presence in every area of life. Take a moment right now and say it aloud from memory. If you get stuck, take some time to look it up and turn those parts of it that are not already a prayer into a prayer about your awareness of God.

RELIGION

David and Uzzah

READ
2 Samuel 6
Chapter 14, pages 143–153

THEME WORD: RELIGION

Most of us who know God experience on almost a daily basis the frustrating transitions back and forth between religion and relationship. We find relationship with our Creator so dynamic and at times terrifying that we often gravitate to false relief in religion—putting God under wraps. Fortunately, God refuses to be managed. If we don't learn that lesson, our efforts to control God may turn out to be self-destructive.

1. What clues remind you that you have strayed into the wilderness of religion and have left that sense of relationship behind?

KEY PASSAGES

Jesus said, "You're tied down to the mundane; I'm in touch with what is beyond your horizons. You live in terms of what you see and touch.

I'm living on other terms. I told you that you were missing God in all this. You're at a dead end. If you won't believe I am who I say I am, you're at the dead end of sins. You're missing God in your lives."
(John 8:23-24)

Exodus 37:1-9
1 Samuel 4:1–7:1
2 Samuel 6
Psalm 132
Matthew 23:27

DAVID'S STORY

2. Who are the main people who inhabit this chapter of Scripture, and how do they shape the story?

3. How did the Ark come to be at the home of Abinadab in Kiriath Jearim? (See 1 Samuel 4:1–7:1.)

4. What were David's two conflicting emotions when Uzzah was killed?

" David wasn't careful with God. When Uzzah died, David lost his temper with God. He saw the death; he didn't see what had led up to it. He had no sense of the years of slow suicide that came to a conclusion beside the ox-cart. All David saw was an interruption to his parade, turning it into a funeral cortege. Angry with God, David went home in a sulk, pouting **"** (pages 151–152).

5. How was Uzzah's presumptive gesture to steady the Ark possibly a result of "the years of slow suicide" that Peterson suggests? (See page 150.)

6. In what ways is getting angry with God a part of being in relationship with him?

7. What changed about David when he returned to retrieve the Ark and bring it to Jerusalem?

" Michal would have been comfortable walking beside the Ark with Uzzah, stately, proper, careful. And dead **"** (page 153).

8. What kind of attitudes did Michal share with Uzzah? Why did they influence her response when she saw her husband dancing before the Lord?

LARGER STORY

" The Ark didn't have magical properties. When the Hebrews treated it (and later the Temple) that way—as a source of power or good luck—the prophets did their best to confront them and face them with the reality of a personal God, as over against an impersonal relic. . . .

The Ark kept all this before them. That was its purpose: to hold up the evidence of the kind of God with whom they had to do. This wasn't a piece of memorabilia but a display of what was going on—what was always going on, what was still going on: God's presence and action among them worked into the material (stone and pottery and wood) of their lives " (pages 148–149).

9. What's the difference between recognizing the holiness of an object or place and making that object or place the thing to be worshipped itself?

10. What are examples of the misleading power of relics and memorabilia today (in buildings, places, objects)?

" Holy Scripture posts Uzzah as a danger sign for us: 'Beware the God.' It's especially important to have such a sign posted in places designated for religious worship and learning **"** (page 150).

11. In what way is Uzzah a blunt warning, and what real tendencies in us does his death warn us about?

12. How does Matthew 23:27 provide a powerful commentary by Jesus on the results of starting off out of reverence for God and ending up trying to manage God?

YOUR STORY

" When we're going about our work responsibly and steadily, we walk. Walking is our normal mode of locomotion. But when we're beside ourselves with love, charged with excess of meaning, shaken out of preoccupation with ourselves, we dance **"** (page 152).

13. Are you familiar with this kind of dancing? When was the last time you were overtaken by the reality of God's majesty to the point of motion?

14. What influences the border around your comfort zone when it comes to expressing yourself before God?

" Worship is the time and place that we assign for deliberate attentiveness to God—not because he's confined to time and place but because our self-importance is so insidiously relentless that if we don't deliberately interrupt ourselves regularly, we have no chance of attending to him at all at other times and in other places " (pages 152–153).

15. What are the regular times you assign yourself for worship? Are they sporadic or do they create a rhythm to your life?

16. When was the last unexpected time of worship that happened in your life in part because of the regularity of your worship pattern?

17. How does Peterson caution us about the necessity to remember, even with healthy worship patterns, that the signs of warning and caution should be posted always in our minds? (See page 153.)

FOR PRAYERFUL REFLECTION

The shock of Uzzah's death makes us particularly uncomfortable if we assume that second chances are a sequence without an end as far as God is concerned. Is the shock because of our compassion for Uzzah or the sudden chill at how easily we might presume to "help" God with one of his projects? If you haven't done this in a while, meditate on the commands in Scripture to "fear the LORD." Ponder how that affects your current interaction with God.

SOVEREIGN GRACE

David and Nathan

READ
2 Samuel 7
Chapter 15, pages 155–167

THEME WORD: SOVEREIGN GRACE

This double term emphasizes several layers of meaning. Grace might be as simple a thing as common courtesy, but making it sovereign raises the bar considerably. Making it sovereign also increases the improbability of it. A sovereign (as God is sovereign) would not have the need to be gracious unless it is a surprising, unexpected, but amazing aspect of the character of the one who is sovereign. That is ultimately who God is—Sovereign!

KEY PASSAGES

"My kingdom," said Jesus, "doesn't consist of what you see around you. If it did, my followers would fight so that I wouldn't be handed over to the Jews. But I'm not that kind of king, not the world's kind of king."

Then Pilate said, "So, are you a king or not?"

Jesus answered, "You tell me. Because I am King, I was born and entered the world so that I could witness to the truth. Everyone who

cares for truth, who has any feeling for the truth, recognizes my voice."
(John 18:36-37)

2 Samuel 7
Psalm 2; 21; 93

DAVID'S STORY

1. Nathan the prophet is abruptly introduced at this point in the
David story. Why does Nathan immediately give his blessing to
David to address the apparent unacceptable situation of the Ark
sitting in a tent?

2. How did God change the blessing that Nathan originally gave
to David?

3. How did God shift the weight of the conversation from tempo-
ral temples to his eternal plan? (See 2 Samuel 7:4-16.)

" David's prayers are steeped in the imagery and conviction of God's
sovereign rule. God's sovereignty is the single most distinctive element
in the belief system that gives coherence to the many and various
prayers that through the centuries were collected and arranged under
David's name in the Psalms " (page 156).

4. Second Samuel 7:18-29 records one of David's prayers. What were the central points that he wanted to express to God?

5. What does David say about God in his prayer and what does he say about himself?

6. How does David distinguish between his own sovereignty and God's?

" Nathan went back to David in the morning and withdrew the building permit. Pastors and prophets and priests also find themselves doing this quite often, and always awkwardly. Why would a prophet of God discourage well-intended work for God? " (page 160).

7. What makes this task of discouraging well-intended work something awkward for Nathan, or any pastor, prophet, or priest?

❝ David *sat*. This may be the single most critical act that David ever did, the action that put him out of action—more critical than killing Goliath, more critical than honoring Saul (his enemy) as God's anointed, more critical than bringing the Ark to Jerusalem. More critical because what David now does in response to Nathan's pastoral/ prophetic counsel will either qualify or disqualify him from the king-work for which he has been anointed, trained, preserved, and empowered ❞ (page 162).

8. What difference can kneeling, sitting, standing, or lying prostrate make? What determines the effectiveness of any of these postures?

9. How was David's response in word and posture the right one?

LARGER STORY

❝ What we don't do for God is often far more critical than what we in fact do. God is the beginning, center, and end of the world's life—of existence itself. But we're often unaware of God's action except dimly and peripherally. Especially when we're in full possession of our powers—our education complete, our careers in full swing, people admiring us and prodding us onward—it's hard not to imagine that we're at the beginning, center, and end of the world, or at least of that part of the world in which we're placed ❞ (pages 163–164).

10. How does not doing for God relate to a biblical phrase like "Be still, and know that I am God" (Psalm 46:10, RSV)?

11. What can we do about "our powers" to keep from trying to apply them independently of God?

" Modern Christians are characteristically much afraid of being caught out doing too little for God, let alone nothing. But there are moments, far more frequent than we suppose, when doing nothing is precisely the gospel thing to do " (page 164).

12. What heresy that distorts the above principle does Peterson warn against? (See page 164.)

13. So, what should be done while we're doing nothing?

YOUR STORY

" There's no danger in such inaction that we'll end up with nothing to do. David did much before he sat down, and he did much afterward: God commands and we obey; God sends and we go. The Christian life is a gloriously active life as the Holy Spirit does the work of Christ in and through us " (page 165).

14. So "being still" is not quite the same as "remaining still." And "silence" is healthy when in rhythm with other responses. As your life is now constituted, how much time are you devoting to being still? Of what does that stillness consist for you?

15. How are "obedience" and "going" combining with "stillness" in your life right now?

FOR PRAYERFUL REFLECTION

Think about your habits of prayer posture. What positions are you not used to assuming before God? Is that a habitual choice or a conscious decision that certain postures, such as kneeling or prostrating, would not be appropriate? Think about how posture emphasizes your ability to be still before God. You may end up sitting.

LOVE

David and Mephibosheth

READ

2 Samuel 9

Chapter 16, pages 169–179

THEME WORD: LOVE

Love is certainly a marvelous experience when it's reciprocal, whether in a marriage or a friendship. But love takes on a special character when it is expressed before and beyond response. God loved us long before we loved him. God loved us despite our efforts not to love him. This love isn't given because the source is needy but because the source realizes even those who don't love need to be loved.

KEY PASSAGES

"Let me give you a new command: Love one another. In the same way I loved you, you love one another. This is how everyone will recognize that you are my disciples—when they see the love you have for each other." (John 13:34-35)

1 Samuel 20:14-15

2 Samuel 4:4; 9; 16–19

DAVID'S STORY

1. Second Samuel 8:15-18 describes a point of stability and calm in David's kingdom. David begins to think about past commitments. At the beginning of 2 Samuel 9, what does he say is his purpose for asking if there are any surviving members of Saul's household?

2. Who alerts David that Jonathan has a surviving son, crippled in both feet? What part does this man later play in the relationship between David and Mephibosheth?

66 Exile communities commonly maintain a sense of identity—pride even—by remembering the former days when they had played a significant role in history, recounting the stories of their displacement and debasement. It's easy enough to imagine Mephibosheth growing up on such stories, told by the servants around late-evening fires in Lo-debar. I'm guessing that his nurse was his primary storyteller and that the stories all contributed in one way or another to a deep sense of victimization 99 (page 170).

3. How is this description confirmed by Mephibosheth's response to David's first words? (See 2 Samuel 9:6-8.)

4. What steps does David take to ensure that Mephibosheth will be cared for?

❝ What Mephibosheth didn't know when he was brought into David's court, and could never have imagined in his wildest dreams, is that he was there to be loved. . . .

What Mephibosheth didn't know was that he was standing before a very different kind of king than the world in which he had grown up had any right to expect ❞ (page 172).

5. Based on cultural cues and family history, what was Mephibosheth expecting?

6. How does 1 Samuel 20:14-15 explain what was motivating David's actions?

❝ David emerges into prominence here as a lover. His kingly rule was already marked by justice and fairness. There is, though, an element without which those qualities aren't complete, and that element is love ❞ (page 173).

7. What is the meaning of *chesed* as a term for love in Hebrew that has special connotations?

8. In what ways is this tested and tried love the one thing we hardly dare to believe we will ever find in the world? How do you imagine this unexpected love affected Mephibosheth? What hints do you find in his story?

LARGER STORY

" Mephibosheth was the son of Jonathan, David's oldest and best friend. Three times in the David cycle his name is brought to our attention. Cumulatively, the three stories embed Mephibosheth in our imaginations in such a way that by now the mere mention of the name to those of us who have entered the David story arouses latent impulses of generosity and channels them into strategies of love in the men and women who commit themselves to live by faith in Jesus Christ " (page 169).

9. How do the episodes in David's life that included Mephibosheth work together to show the various sides of David's love?

10. After reading the account in 2 Samuel 16–19 of Ziba's actions during Absalom's rebellion, what do you conclude about his version of events compared to Mephibosheth's?

11. Entirely apart from Mephibosheth's response to David's love, how do you explain the powerful motivation toward generosity that this episode provokes in Christians?

" Any of these responses to David's love is conceivable, and the narrator doesn't make it absolutely clear which is true. The ambiguity is intentional, for we mustn't suppose that there are any guarantees that a generous act of love will be rewarded by loyal gratitude. Not all, not even most, love is requited. We need to be realistic about what's involved in living out covenantal love. It's a risky business. We can be taken advantage of; we can be betrayed. Jesus was and is. David may have been **"** (page 176).

12. Why is unrequited covenant love still worth exercising?

13. Why does Peterson note that when it comes to covenant love, Jesus was and is taken advantage of and betrayed? What does he mean?

YOUR STORY

❝ And then we come before God, a God of power and mystery. How will he treat us? Will he punish us, destroy us, take away our freedom? Based on our experience, any of that is certainly possible, maybe even probable. That's why we need so much reassurance: 'Relax. It's going to be all right.' The phrase is often on the lips of angels, the emissaries of God's good news. It was often on the lips of Jesus, who regularly brought frightened and bewildered men and women into the very presence of God. Here it's on David's lips ❞ (page 175).

14. How are we like Mephibosheth when we come before God? What is our condition?

15. In what ways do you respond to God's assurance that it's going to be all right? Why do you believe that?

❝ And I love this story of David and Mephibosheth because I continue to catch glimpses of it and hear echoes of it in stories in which I have a part ❞ (page 179).

16. How does Peterson explain this statement? How have you found the same thing to be true in your own experience?

FOR PRAYERFUL REFLECTION

In the Gospels, four men bring a paralyzed man to Jesus for healing. The need is painfully obvious. Yet Jesus looks at him and says, "I forgive your sins" (Mark 2:5). He healed him deeply before he healed his body. When Jesus looks at you today, what's the first thing he says to you?

SIN

David and Bathsheba

READ

2 Samuel 11–12

Chapter 17, pages 181–191

THEME WORD: SIN

Far more often than we readily agree, sin has nothing to do with sex. But sometimes, it does. But even when it does, sex outside of God's beautiful design usually turns out to be just the tip of the sin iceberg. Missing the mark, falling short, and deliberately disobeying what we know God wants us to do—sin. David was a sinner. Then again, so are we.

1. Given what you know of David and Bathsheba, which one of the two do you most closely identify with? Why?

KEY PASSAGES

Jesus stood up and spoke to her. . . . "Does no one condemn you?"
"No one, Master."

"Neither do I," said Jesus. "Go on your way. From now on, don't sin." (John 8:10-11)

Genesis 3:4-5
2 Samuel 11–12
Psalm 51
Malachi 4:4

DAVID'S STORY

2. Reading this account for yourself in 2 Samuel 11–12, what strikes you the most about David's actions?

3. Until Nathan shows up on the scene, is there any evidence that David is troubled by what he has done? What "God moments" along the way could have changed David's course?

❝ In the encounter with Bathsheba, David recovers his identity as a person of prayer. But this story is more complex, for this time around David is no longer fresh and innocent; he's been scarred in many a battle, is experienced in failure and disappointment. God is no less a part of his life, but the life itself is now multilayered, carrying in it tangled and intermingled complexities of guilt and grace ❞ (page 182).

4. Do the complexities of a situation affect the level of culpability for choices made, or do they simply allow us to see the tangled mess created by different people's overlapping choices?

5. What do we learn about the use and impact of the word *sent* in this episode? (See pages 183–184.)

6. To what degree would you say that Bathsheba was a full participant in this series of sinful decisions?

66 David is now in gospel focus. Addressed personally, he answers personally: 'I have sinned against the Lord' (2 Sam. 12:13 [RSV]). He abandons the generalities of religion. He quits giving out opinions on other people's lives, good or bad, realizes his position before God—a sinner! A person in trouble, a person who needs help, a human being who needs God 99 (page 185).

7. What does Nathan accomplish by telling David a story rather than accusing him of sin?

8. Given the typical response to the news of one's sinfulness, how is David's immediate response quite different than what a human would normally say? Why is this?

LARGER STORY

" In the Christian life our primary task isn't to *avoid* sin, which is impossible anyway, but to *recognize* sin. The fact is that we're sinners. But there's an enormous amount of self-deception in sin. When this is combined with devil-deception, the task of recognition is compounded " (page 186).

9. What is supposed to happen when we recognize sin? Can David's response when he finally recognized sin be a good guideline for us? Why?

10. Given what we've learned in this book so far, what would be Peterson's recommendation for dealing with the double deceptions of self and the devil?

" There's a remarkable verbal resonance to this story of David standing before Nathan in that of Jesus standing before Pilate. They're both passion stories—David's passion for Bathsheba; Jesus' passion for us. Pilate says of Jesus, 'Behold the man' (John 19:5 [RSV]), echoing what Nathan says to David, 'You are the man' **"** (page 190).

11. In what way are both Pilate's and Nathan's statements profoundly true?

12. Why was it crucial for the world to find out that Jesus was "the man" and why was it life-giving for David to discover he was the man?

YOUR STORY

" This is the gospel focus: *you* are the man; *you* are the woman. The gospel is never about somebody else; it's always about you, about me. The gospel is never a truth in general; it's always a truth in specific. The gospel is never a commentary on ideas or culture or conditions; it's always about actual persons, actual pain, actual trouble, actual sin: you, me; who you are and what you've done; who I am and what I've done **"** (page 185).

13. What places in your life allow you the freedom to confess that you are a sinner? What places seem to conspire to keep you from facing that fact?

14. How important do you think it is for you to spend time with people who know you as a sinner and recognize God's love for you in spite of that fact?

" Our sins aren't that interesting; it's God's work that's interesting. There's nothing glamorous about sin, and it's the devil's work to make it look otherwise. Sin is diminishing, dehumanizing, and soon dull. After it's been recognized and confessed, the less said about it the better **"** (page 190).

15. What does the phrase "it's God's work that's interesting" mean to you?

16. How does Peterson spell out the way to handle confession under the Psalm 51 model? (See page 190.)

FOR PRAYERFUL REFLECTION

Psalm 51 is a humbling, crushing, vulnerable, and hopeful psalm. If you have not read it recently, do so. If you haven't prayed it recently, ask yourself if you might not be living under a cloud of self- and devil-deception.

SUFFERING

David and Absalom

READ

2 Samuel 16–18

Chapter 18, pages 193–204

THEME WORD: SUFFERING

Suffering is generally a word we avoid almost as much as we try to avoid that to which it refers. We might be willing to talk about suffering; we're not nearly as willing to walk through places of suffering. But suffering comes. And God uses suffering. But whatever good comes out of suffering doesn't diminish the fact that suffering is the hard place in life.

   1. How would you explain to someone that you know what suffering is?

KEY PASSAGES

At noon the sky became extremely dark. The darkness lasted three hours. At three o'clock, Jesus groaned out of the depths, crying loudly, "Eloi,

Eloi, lama sabachthani?" *which means, "My God, my God, why have you abandoned me?"* (Mark 15:33-34)

2 Samuel 16–18
Psalm 55

DAVID'S STORY

2. David saw something he wanted and took it, not considering what would happen next. How did his son Amnon repeat the same sin?

3. In what different ways did David fail each of his children that were involved in the events in these chapters?

4. How was this a fulfillment of Nathan's words to David in 2 Samuel 12:7-10?

" This is the third monumental sin of David's life, the most inexcusable, and the one for which he paid the most. The adultery with Bathsheba was the affair of a passionate moment. The murder of Uriah was a royal reflex to avoid detection. But the rejection of Absalom was a steady, determined refusal to share with his son what God had so abundantly shared with him. Day by day he hardened in this denial of love. This was sin with a blueprint. This was sin that required long-term commitment, comprehensive strategy. Jerusalem was a small city: scrupulous care was necessary to avoid seeing or being seen by Absalom **" (page 197).

5. How would you describe David's method of parental discipline? What do you think he would have said if someone had asked him, "David, what are you thinking?"

6. What made this treatment of Absalom the most inexcusable of David's sins?

" In suffering, David recovered humility. He got back in touch with himself—his basic, elemental self. He recovered humility when Shimei cursed him (2 Sam. 16:5-14 [RSV]). . . .

In suffering, David recovered prayer. He got in personal touch again with his personal God. David recovered prayer when he learned that Ahithophel had betrayed him. . . .

In suffering, David recovered compassion—he got in touch with his long-estranged son Absalom. He recovered his extraordinary capacity to love **"** (pages 198–199, 202).

7. How does the story describe each of these recoveries? What did David lose in the process?

8. How does David's eventual lament for Absalom echo David's lament for Saul and Jonathan earlier? How do these laments acknowledge the things that can't be changed but must be left in God's hands?

LARGER STORY

" I pause and reflect how differently this story would have turned out if David had anticipated the story Jesus told about the father whose son went into a far country, lived a life of self-indulgence, and returned having disgraced his father's house. Even though the son had done a terrible thing, the father never quit looking for him, looking for a way to forgive him, restore him to full sonship. When he did come, finally, the father ran to greet and embrace him, welcoming him home with a huge banquet (Luke 15:11-32 [RSV]) " (pages 196–197).

9. What would have been required for the prodigal son scenario to work out in David's life?

10. In a breakdown of the father-son relationship, both parties bear responsibility, but which party bears the greater duty of the first move in the right direction? How does the prodigal son story illustrate this?

" Back in the wilderness, where so much of David's character had been formed, we now see him recovering that which is, well, so *characteristically* David. Hardship brings out the best in David. Suffering can, if we let it, make us better instead of worse " (page 198).

11. Can you envision a person's life ever getting to the place this side of eternity where more time in the wilderness might not be required anymore? Why is wilderness always a possibility around the next bend in the road?

YOUR STORY

12. When was your last trip into the wilderness and what did you recover or learn there?

13. Who has served in your life the way Shimei served in David's? Though Shimei's intent wasn't to encourage David, how did his cursing end up confirming the principle already in place stated in Romans 8:28? How was God working for good even though David's world was collapsing around him?

14. In Jesus' story of the prodigal, with whom do you identify: the father, the son, or the older brother? How has God reached you where you are?

" Loving Absalom that day was one of the most magnificent things David ever did. . . .

In this lament, at the farthest descent from Jerusalem, deep in the wilderness forest of Ephraim, David's story most clearly anticipates and most nearly approximates the gospel story, the story of Jesus that now extends into our stories. Passion stories. Stories of suffering—but suffering that neither diminishes nor destroys us but makes us more human, praying and loving " (page 204).

15. What good has come out of suffering for you? What lessons have you learned in the wilderness times that you know you would have never learned anywhere else?

FOR PRAYERFUL REFLECTION

David's three-way wilderness recovery involved humanity, prayer, and love—results often derived from times in dry country. Perhaps having your life overthrown isn't necessary, but asking God to show you the condition of your life in these three areas might cause you to embark with him on a walk into a wilderness place in your soul.

THEOLOGY

David and God

READ

2 Samuel 22

Chapter 19, pages 205–216

THEME WORD: THEOLOGY

The traditional definition of theology takes the Greek underlying words and paraphrases them as *words about God*. David takes theology in a direction few others followed, but from which countless have benefited. His theology was more often *words to God*. And then in a way that sometimes escapes us as we look at the printed page, we have to be reminded that for David, these were *songs to God*.

1. If your life were to be a theological expression right now, what would it be?

KEY PASSAGES

I came so they can have real and eternal life, more and better life than they ever dreamed of. (John 10:10)

2 Samuel 22
Psalm 18

DAVID'S STORY

2. Second Samuel 19–21 offers a review of many events in David's reign that were not specifically described elsewhere. Life was winding down. As if to create a conclusion fitting for David, the book closes with his song from which this book takes its title, *Leap Over a Wall*. What walls in David's story have left the deepest impression on your mind?

3. David not only celebrated God in his songs, he expressed a range of emotions that can only be verified by a lifetime of visits to the Psalms where we repeatedly discover in the words of these songs the very choruses and verses that have been echoing, perhaps with less experienced words, in our hearts. Which psalms are on your go-to list, and why?

66 The single most characteristic thing about David is God. David believed in God, thought about God, imagined God, addressed God, prayed to God. The larger part of David's existence wasn't David but God.

The evidence for David's pervasive, saturated awareness of God is in his profusion of metaphors: bedrock, castle, knight, crag, boulders, hideout. David was immersed in God. Every visibility revealed for him an invisibility. David named God by metaphor 99 (pages 206–207).

4. What do you think a life whose single most characteristic thing is God is supposed to look like on a day-to-day basis? Is it a perfect life or is it something else entirely?

5. As you read through Psalm 18:1-7 (see page 206), as David speaks about God, what is he saying about himself?

66 David characteristically uses words magnificently. He uses words to sing and to pray. He uses words to mint reality, fresh and shining. David is a poet—which is to say, he uses words to *make* something, not just talk about something 99 (page 209).

6. Take your time reading Psalm 18:8-20 (see page 208). What line or phrase captures your imagination as you think about God? How would you echo that line in your own words?

7. On page 209, what do you make of Peterson's claim that "All of us are poets to begin with"?

" The David story is a gospel story. God doing for David what David could never do for himself. A sinner saved. It's a story that gets completed in the Jesus story, which features God seeking the sick, the rejected, and the lost " (page 211).

8. Pages 210–211 include verses 21-28 of Psalm 18. How does the rhythm switch from writer to God and back? How does David celebrate his responsive role?

9. The last section of Psalm 18 fills much of pages 212–216. How are these flowing phrases a testimony to all that God has done in and for David?

LARGER STORY

" God doesn't reveal reality so that we can stand around and look at it as spectators but so that we can enter it and become at home in it. Language is a primary way in which we come to be 'at home.' As we learn language, we're finding out not so much what's there but where we are; we're learning the neighborhood and finding the words that connect us with what and who is there " (page 209).

10. How does language influence your relationship with God? What words do you use that are reserved for use when you've got God in mind?

11. In what ways does this quote shed light on John 1:1,14 and the biblical claim that Jesus is the Word?

“ There wasn't much of life left unexplored or unattended by David. And always—or at least eventually—the largest part of life for him was God. If we're not adoring, believing, and obeying, we miss out on most of what's right before our eyes ” (page 216).

12. God's omniscience and omnipresence mean that there's nowhere we can explore that is unfamiliar to God. David's boldness in living before God makes him an example of one of those who have gone where few have gone before. What do you think it took to be that kind of person?

13. What is the difference between affirming that God knows us inside out on the one hand and inviting God to know us (as he already does)? What does the welcome say about relationship?

YOUR STORY

" David with all his rough edges. He never got around to loving his enemies the way his descendant Jesus would do it; his morals and manners left a lot to be desired. These aren't narrated as blemishes, however, but as conditions that we share. They aren't narrated to legitimize bad behavior but are set down as proof that we don't first become good and then get God. First we get God—and then, over a patient lifetime, we're trained in God's ways " (page 216).

14. One difference between David and most of us is that he rarely made an effort to hide his rough edges. He lived in plain sight. What were the benefits of such a life?

15. Several times Peterson has pointed out that David was not a moral model to be followed or imitated in the details, but his relationship with God deserves our attention. How do the rough edges in your life affect your relationship with God? Are those the places you meet God or hide from him?

FOR PRAYERFUL REFLECTION

This might be a good time to start working on a psalm for your life. What do you want people who know you to know about your life in God? What kind of written record would you like to leave of the great thing God has been able to accomplish in, around, and in spite of you?

CHAPTER 20

DEATH

David and Abishag

READ
1 Kings 1–2
Chapter 20, pages 217–229

THEME WORD: DEATH

Death might be seen as a good way to end the story if death was the end of the story—but it isn't. When people accept the lights out lie as a description of death they miss the grand banquet for which life on this side of eternity is merely the appetizer. But when death is birth into life as we've never known it, we can start dealing with death honestly, as a real experience for which to prepare, in which to enter with our eyes wide open, and in which we can be present with others as they are transposed into eternity.

KEY PASSAGES

Listen carefully: Unless a grain of wheat is buried in the ground, dead to the world, it is never any more than a grain of wheat. But if it is buried, it sprouts and reproduces itself many times over. In the same way, anyone who holds on to life just as it is destroys that life. But if you let it go, reckless in your love, you'll have it forever, real and eternal. (John 12:24-25)

1 Kings 1–2
Psalm 22

DAVID'S STORY

1. As you read through the first two chapters of 1 Kings, what is the cast of characters that inhabit David's story at the end? Why is each of them there?

2. Who was with David when he died?

3. David had some final words for Solomon. Which of these instructions are wise and hopeful, which ones should have been left unsaid?

66 But when David died, no one at all lamented him, let alone magnificently. He died in the middle of a family squabble, with no hint of either tribute or eulogy. Instead of dying in peace, with his children and wives gathered around him expressing love and gratitude, he was embroiled in a mare's nest of intrigue and deceit. And it wasn't only what others were doing; David himself contributed his share to the general messiness of the occasion **99** (page 218).

4. Based on 1 Kings 2:10, what do we know about David's funeral arrangements? What does this hint about those who were closest to him at the end?

" Abishag is the one bright spot in the darkness and chaos surrounding David's deathbed. Abishag, in contrast to everyone else at this time, is present only to serve, content only to serve. She has no ambitions to fulfill, nothing she's scheming to get from David. Her only qualifications are nonfunctional: her beauty and her youth " (pages 218–219).

5. How often is Abishag mentioned in these chapters? Because she was silently present at most of the proceedings, what do you think was her perspective of David's life?

" Responsible Bathsheba makes David responsible. Because of Bathsheba's concern and intervention, the Davidic kingdom continues without interruption into the Solomonic kingdom " (page 224).

6. Peterson follows this observation with notes on three different storylines that David's death includes: a political story, a theological story, and a David story. Identify each of these and consider how God made use of them.

7. Does God require the intervention of people like Bathsheba (or us), or does he always have ways to get things done according to his will?

LARGER STORY

" I object to the reduction of Abishag to a function. In the story as it's given to us, she's something far more: a witness to the sanctity of death, a sacred presence to David in his dying—and as such a quiet rebuke to the others in the story who respond to David's death as either a problem to be solved, an opportunity to be seized, or a difficulty to be negotiated " (page 219).

8. Who represents each of these ways of handling death in David's story?

9. How might each of these approaches be identified in those attending to someone's death today?

" The more we deal with death as a problem, the more we—as onlookers—can be useful and 'alive,' spend our energy and money searching, buying, commanding. Thus involved, we never have to look the dying person in the eyes, wipe her tears, listen to his confession, honor this life, just as it is. The only difference between David's servants and so many of us is that we have more options, more technology, and more incentive to distract us from the person who is dying.

But Abishag, even though failed as a cure, stays on as a person " (page 220).

10. Hospice care is a practical way for families to find some assistance as they cope with the declining health of a loved one. What are the real benefits? In what ways might there be drawbacks to employing the help of those outside of the family?

11. If death shouldn't be seen as a problem, opportunity, or difficulty, how should it be seen? To what degree can we serve as Abishag to those we love?

YOUR STORY

" These three responses continue to be common among us. One of the hardest things about dying is having to deal with people who don't know how to behave in the presence of death, who lose all sense of what it means to be a human being with limits, who under the provocations of death forget how to live and love, who flee from the mystery of death and in so doing desert the dying person. If death doesn't teach us how to live as humans (instead of attempting to be gods), it can only be feared or denied for as long as possible. But if it becomes a way to face limits and define the humanity proper to us, both death and each individual's dying can be accepted and even embraced ” (page 219).

12. What could you do to ensure that you understand "how to behave in the presence of death"? Who do you know who has these skills?

13. When was the last time you had a conversation with those closest to you about the subject of death and inquired honestly about their thoughts on the unavoidable coming experience for us all? How are you prepared to speak about resurrection hope?

14. Based on the lessons from Abishag, what changes might you have to make about your plans for your own death and your willingness to enter into the experiences of those around you?

" The David story doesn't trade in illusion and doesn't sentimentalize. The Christian life isn't a romantic idyll, and those who say otherwise deceive us. What we need more than anything is a detailed acquaintance with and feel for the reality of a life that's truly and deeply human, a humanity in which death is both basic experience and pervasive metaphor. This David story as it's given to us does just that, preparing us to live the Jesus life that finally, but only finally, yields to resurrection " (page 224).

15. How has this time spent in David's story helped prepare you to live the Jesus life with more integrity, anticipation, and joy?

FOR PRAYERFUL REFLECTION

The final pages of *Leap Over a Wall* lead us through a reflection on the death and resurrection of Jesus, particularly as anticipated in Psalm 22. Before you end this study, reread that section (on pages 224–228) prayerfully. The final wall we have to leap in this life is the death wall, and only with God's help can we hope to make that jump!

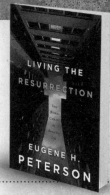

The Message Means Understanding

Bringing the Bible to all ages

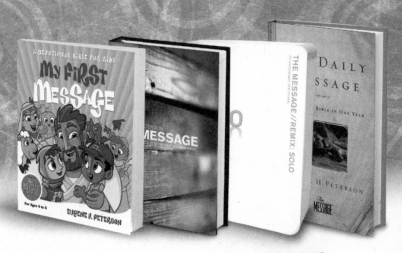

The Message is written in contemporary language that is much like talking with a good friend. When paired with your favorite Bible study, *The Message* will deliver a reading experience that is reliable, energetic, and amazingly fresh.

To find *The Message* that is right for you, go to **www.navpress.com** or call **1-800-366-7788**.

NAVPRESS
Discipleship Inside Out™

Discover What the Bible Really Says
LifeChange by The Navigators

The LifeChange Bible study series can help you grow in Christlikeness through a life-changing encounter with God's Word. Discover what the Bible says—not what someone else thinks it says—and develop the skills and desire to dig even deeper into God's Word. Each study includes study aids and discussion questions.

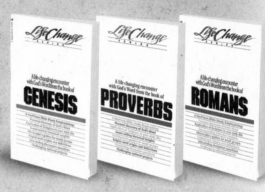